MW01088501

THE PASTOR'S HANDBOOK

A book of forms and instructions for
conducting the many ceremonies which constitute
the pastoral function,
published in collaboration with
the Division of Church Ministries
of The Christian and Missionary Alliance

Christian Publications

Camp Hill, Pennsylvania

Christian Publications

3825 Hartzdale Drive, Camp Hill, PA 17011

The mark of ✝ vibrant faith

ISBN: 0-87509-118-0

CONTENTS

PREFACE

"To know what to say and how to say it . . . what finer gift could a clergyman possess?"— CHARLES PERKINS.

The PASTOR'S HANDBOOK is intended to meet a continuous need among ministers for forms and guidance in the performance of their varied services. While it may not accommodate itself to all, it is well adapted to the practice of the ministry generally.

The formulas are sufficient for the ordinary needs of ministerial life and may be modified or extended as desired. Supplemental materials from the pastor's private collection, or those of his own preparation, may easily be typed and inserted ·into the loose-leaf arrangement. The book is intended to be as flexible as a man's personal preference while at the same time a guide with forms of quality, beauty, and dignity.

Set forms of devotion are disliked by some who prefer a simple mode of worship and who stress spiritual liberty in prayer and preaching. There need be no fear of these forms becoming lifeless ritual as long as the spiritual vitality of a church is maintained. The use of necessary forms should never become merely formal. And if the use of such forms adds beauty and dignity to the atmosphere of sacredness, who can object?

May the blessing of God attend all who glean here, enabling them to know what to say and how to say it; what to do and how to do it, as occasions may require.

[5]

THE MINISTER

The minister touches those who wait on his ministry in their most solemn and sacred moments. Whether the dedication of a young life, the uniting in matrimony of trustful youth or the burial of the aged—great responsibility rests on the servant of the Lord. How best can these high and holy obligations be discharged? This is at once the question of every earnest and thoughtful minister.

First, let the minister watch his spirit. Professionalism, like spiritual decline, begins in the heart. Nothing is so important as heart-interest in the spiritual welfare of those who look to the minister for help. The service, whatever its nature, signifies much to those for whom it is held. No ceremony is meaningless to those whose hearts are touched by its observance. Since it is important to those for whom it is conducted, it must be important to him who conducts it. Carelessness in the clergyman here will beget a callousness in others that will render the service ineffectual. If it becomes "just another service" then no healing helpfulness is possible.

Let the minister be careful about his personal appearance. Upon the occasions herein covered, the minister, whatever the limitations of his wardrobe, is to be conservatively attired. The best dressed are always modestly garbed and the cut and color of the minister's clothes should enhance the dignity of his calling. Clothes may not make the man but they have been the unmaking of some ministers. Pens and pencils should be kept in an inside pocket. Nothing on or about the minister is to clamor for attention. Cleanliness may not be next to godliness but it ranks nearby. The sacred injunction, "Be ye clean that bear the vessels of the Lord," is capable of wide application. Offense by lack of cleanliness is never excusable.

The minister must see to his manner. Gravity need not be gloom and seriousness is not necessarily sadness. The minister's manner will reflect the importance of the occasion. The King's business calls for a kingly bearing and he who represents another should act as befits that one. The refined are never noisy. Quiet reserve is always the mark of a Christian gentleman. The rough and rude handling to which many a service is subjected often ruins its helpfulness. To be late, light, or long is to spoil our opportunity and mar the occasion. The pastor should act in such a way that none shall ever regret having sought his assistance. Manner is the sum total of manners.

Brethren, we are called to be good ministers of Jesus Christ. No man could be more; who dares to be less?

THE WEDDING

INTRODUCTION

A wedding ceremony should be as sacred as a communion service. Couples should be impressed that it is a covenant between them which is witnessed by God. The union of Christ with His Church, and her subjection to Him, underlie the very relationship of marriage and afford the pattern for every godly union. Therefore, in this day of moral decay and disintegration of the marriage bond, everything that would obscure its sacred character and binding influence must be steadfastly resisted.

The servant of God should ascertain the fitness

of the parties to be married, bearing in mind particularly the scriptural restraint on the marriage of divorced persons and those who would be "unequally yoked" together. Tactfully handled, the act of refusing to perform a marriage ceremony need not prove embarrassing, and if the reasons are stated kindly an opportunity to give spiritual counsel is sometimes afforded. But, embarrassing or not, a minister is under no obligation to marry those who do not measure up to the scriptural standards which he has been ordained to uphold.

Laws governing the performance of the marriage ceremony vary in different states and provinces. Let the minister be sure he is thoroughly acquainted with prevailing laws before performing a ceremony. Marriages solemnized under circumstances where the minister has failed to comply with such laws are usually considered valid, but the minister himself is subject to legal penalty and censure. Where reports of marriages are to be made to authorities, or where forms are to be completed and returned, be sure this is done promptly and properly in order to protect the good name and legal record of the parties concerned. Likewise, see that entry of the ceremony is made in the records of the church. A certificate or a booklet, inscribed with the facts of the occasion, is generally given by the minister to the contracting parties.

The pastor should arrange a pre-marriage conference with the young couple requesting his service, at which time he will discuss with them the following:

> (a) The sacredness of the marriage and its continuing bond.

(b) The mutual adjustments necessary for a happy marriage.

(c) The preservation in the married life of the love, thoughtfulness, and mutual understanding of the courtship.

(d) Preparation for the physical aspects of married life, either by referral to the family physician, or competent and well-written books.

(e) An understanding about finances, household expense, savings, and tithing.

(f) Spiritual counsel as to the place Christ shall have in the heart, home, and life; also the establishment of the family altar, observance of the Lord's day and regular attendance at church.

Additional matters may be included as experience and discretion may dictate. Ample time should be allowed to make the conference meaningful and thorough.

It is the bride's prerogative, generally, to plan her wedding as she wants it. Her plans and wishes should be gone over quite thoroughly by the pastor before rehearsal. He will be prepared to offer advice on whatever matters his advice is sought, but he will wisely refrain from proposing changes unless there is some serious infringement on propriety, sanctity of the premises, or established local custom. At the rehearsal he will be in charge of tactfully carrying out the bride's plans, even though numerous changes may be proposed by well-meaning friends. The rehearsal is the time when every participant learns what he is to do and when he is to do it. This includes singers, organist, and ushers, as well as the bridal party.

Books on etiquette will give ample instruction to the ushers for proper seating of the guests. The processional may vary somewhat, due to the number of attendants, arrangement of church aisles, and plans of the bride. Generally, at a prearranged signal the minister, groom, best man and ushers will make their appearance in that order coming in from a side room, and take their places at the altar. The minister will stand in the center and the others at his left, facing the guests. (Sometimes the bride will want the ushers to walk down the aisle with the bridesmaids, or even separately, and take their places at the front.) Next will come the bridesmaids, maid of honor, ring bearer and/or flower girls, and the bride on the left arm of her father or friend. These will take their places at the altar to the right of the minister, the first standing farthest away, the next closer, until finally the bride and her father will be standing directly in front of the minister. (Note: In most areas it is customary for the guests to rise at the appearance of the minister or at the entry of the bridal party, and remain standing throughout the processional. When the bride has reached the altar, the minister will indicate that the guests are to be seated.) The order of the recessional is just the reverse of the processional. The minister may either walk out with the party as it retires, or remain standing at the altar until their exit. He may then retire to the room from whence he entered.

This additional word of counsel might be heeded. Suggest to the bride that she have the florist arrive two or three hours in advance of the time of the ceremony to do his final decorating. This will give the custodian a chance to give the premises a quick "once over" before the last minute. Also suggest to the bride that she inform the photographer that no pictures are to be taken during the ceremony itself. Picture taking may be tolerated up through the processional and begin again with the recessional, but should not be permitted during the ceremony itself. Scenes of the ceremony can be posed afterward.

The nervous and fidgety minister will beget a nervous bridal party. Let him be so familiar with all the particulars that he can impart calmness and inspire confidence. Once the party senses that he is in full command of the situation they will do their part without mistakes. Should a mistake occur, scarcely anyone will notice it if the minister does not become confused. All he needs to do is give calm instruction or prompting just as though that was what the ceremony called for him to do at that point and equilibrium will be maintained.

A COMPLETE WEDDING CEREMONY

When everyone is in readiness before him, the minister may say:

"Let us pray." *(brief invocation)*

"And now ＿＿＿＿＿＿＿, the Scriptures
(Groom's first name)

say to the husband:

'Husbands, love your wives, even as Christ also loved the church, and gave himself for it; that he might present it to himself a glorious church, not having spot, or wrinkle, or any such thing; but that it should be holy and without blemish. So ought men to love their wives.'

"And _____, the Scriptures say

(Bride's first name)

to the wife:

'Wives, submit yourselves unto your own husbands, as unto the Lord. For the husband is the head of the wife, even as Christ is the head of the church; and he is the saviour of the body. Therefore as the church is subject unto Christ, so let the wives be to their own husbands in everything.'

"And to you both the Scriptures say:

'Submitting yourselves one to another in the fear of God.'

"God has so united matrimony with human life, that a man's deepest interest revolves around it. When a man and a woman have chosen each other and come to that moment when they sincerely and publicly join in this covenant for life, they lay down on the altar a holy sacrifice to God, to each other, and to humanity. Thus, they follow God's order and in His ways find true happiness.

"The union into which you are now about to enter, dear friends, is the closest and tenderest into which human beings can come. It is a union founded upon mutual experi-

ence and affection, and to believers in the
Lord Jesus Christ, it is a union in the Lord.
Marriage is God's institution, intended for
the happiness and welfare of mankind.

"We are informed by the Word of God
that:

'Charity suffereth long, and is kind;
Charity envieth not;
Charity vaunteth not itself, is not puffed up,
Doth not behave itself unseemly,
Seeketh not her own,
Is not easily provoked, thinketh no evil;
Rejoiceth not in iniquity,
But rejoiceth in the truth;
Beareth all things, believeth all things,
Hopeth all things, endureth all things.
Charity never faileth.'

"A union embodying such ideals is not to
be entered into lightly or unadvisedly, but
reverently, discreetly, soberly, and in the fear
of God. Into such a union you come now to
be joined."

*(If the bride is to be given in marriage by
her father or guardian, the minister shall ask:)*

"Who giveth _____, to be
                          (Bride's full name)

married to _____?"
                          (Groom's full name)

The father shall answer: "I do." *(Or he
may say:* "Her mother and I.") *He shall*

*place the bride's hand in the groom's hand,
and then be seated.*

"Before the Omniscient God, and in the
presence of these witnesses, wilt thou _____

_____ take _____ here
(Groom's full name)   (Bride's full name)

present, to be thy wedded wife? Wilt thou
love and comfort her, honor and keep her,
and in joy and sorrow, preserve with her this
bond, holy and unbroken, until the coming
of our Lord Jesus Christ, or God by death
shall separate you?" *(The groom should be
instructed in advance to respond by saying,*
"I will.")

"Before the Omniscient God, and in the
presence of these witnesses, wilt thou _____

_____ take _____ here
(Bride's full name)   (Groom's full name)

present, to be thy wedded husband? Wilt
thou love and comfort him, honor and keep
him, and in joy and sorrow, preserve with
him this bond, holy and unbroken, until the
coming of our Lord Jesus Christ, or God by
death shall separate you?" *(The bride should
be instructed in advance to respond by saying,* "I will.")

*(The following exchange of spoken vows
may be omitted if there seems to be sufficient
reason. However, it seems to be more per-*

*sonal and sacred when each speaks his vow
to the other.)*

*Facing his bride and holding her by the
right hand, the man shall say: (either from
memory, or following the minister phrase by
phrase.)*

"I _____, take thee _____
     (Groom's first name)   (Bride's

_____ to be my wedded wife; to love
first name)

thee with all my heart's affection;
to endow thee with all my earthly possessions;
to give thee all the honor of my name;
and to share with thee the grace of my God."

*Facing the groom and holding him by the
right hand, the woman shall say: (either from
memory, or following the minister phrase by
phrase.)*

"I _____, take thee _____
     (Bride's first name)   (Groom's

_____ to be my wedded husband;
first name)

whither thou goest, I will go;
where thou lodgest, I will lodge;
thy people shall be my people,
and thy God shall be my God."

"As a token of this covenant, you will now
give and receive the marriage ring(s)."

*(Make it plural for a double ring ceremony.)
The rings are now to be placed. The best*

man will hand to the groom the ring, which he will place on the ring finger of the woman's left hand. If there is to be a second ring, the maid of honor will hand it to the bride, which she will then place on the ring finger of the man's left hand.

"The unbroken circle, the emblem of eternity, and the gold, the emblem of that which is least tarnished and most enduring, are to show how lasting and imperishable is the faith now mutually pledged by the giving and receiving of this ring (these rings). With this emblem (these emblems) of purity and endless devotion, you do each the other wed, and these marriage vows you do here and now forever seal.

"Let us pray." *This is the prayer of dedication. It is preferable that they kneel, and if desired, while kneeling a song may be sung, followed by prayer.*

"Inasmuch as you _____ and you
(Groom's first name)

_____ have thus consented in holy
(Bride's first name)

wedlock, and have witnessed the same before God and these friends, by virtue of the authority that is vested in me as a minister of the Word of God, and by the laws of this commonwealth, I do now pronounce you husband and wife, united in the pure and holy bonds of wedlock, and those whom God

2

hath joined together let not man put asunder."

(The embrace and kiss may follow.)

"Henceforth, you go down life's pathway together. Let love be the charmed word in all your relationships, and may the circle(s) of your ring(s) typify your unending happiness. May Christ be the Head of your home, the Unseen Guest at every meal, and the Silent Listener to every conversation. May heaven's constant benediction crown your union with ever increasing joy and blessedness and unite your hearts and lives by the grace and true affection of a happy marriage.

" 'The Lord bless thee, and keep thee; the Lord make his face shine upon thee, and be gracious unto thee; the Lord lift up his countenance upon thee, and give thee peace.' In the name of the Father, and of the Son, and of the Holy Ghost. Amen!" *This is the proper place for the pastor to extend congratulations and then introduce the new bridegroom and bride, using the groom's name.* "May I present Mr. and Mrs. John Doe!"

Recessional.

AN ALTERNATE WEDDING CEREMONY

"Jesus, His mother, and His disciples gladly responded to the wedding invitation to witness and participate in the happiness of

the occasion. It was there that He began
His ministry of power, adding to the plea-
sure of those assembled. Thus we come to
witness the vows and pledges _____,
(Groom's first name)

and _____ are to make to each other,
(Bride's first name)

and to participate in the happiness of the
occasion, sending them forth in their new
estate of wedlock with our prayers and Christian greetings.

"You _____, and you _____,
(Groom's first name)   (Bride's first name)

come now to be united in this rite of marriage, which is the first and oldest rite in
the world. It was instituted by God Himself, and the first marriage was performed
by Him. Thus it becomes you to realize the
sacred bonds by which you are united. Although man has fallen, marriage has not fall-
en. It is that part of man's original relationship to God which continues on to bless and
to bring happiness. You will discover that
comfort and happiness in your marriage if
you have it in your hearts to beautify your
relationship with tenderness, thoughtfulness,
patience, kindness and carefulness in the
many ways in which you will be able to be
self-sacrificing, each to the other. And I now
solemnly charge you to remember that it is
just such a commitment of self to each other

which God expects you to make in the
pledges which you make each to the other.

"And now, _____, to the husband

(Groom's first name)

the Scriptures say:

'Husbands, love your wives, even as Christ
also loved the church, and gave himself
for it; That he might present it to himself
a glorious church, not having spot, or
wrinkle, or any such thing; but that it
should be holy and without blemish. So
ought men to love their wives.'

"And _____, to the wife the Scrip-

(Bride's first name)

tures say:

'Wives, submit yourselves unto your own
husbands, as unto the Lord. For the husband is the head of the wife, even as
Christ is the head of the church: and he
is the saviour of the body. Therefore as
the church is subject unto Christ, so let
the wives be to their own husbands in
everything.'

"And, to you both the Scriptures say:

'Submitting yourselves one to another in
the fear of God.'

" _____, do you take _____

(Groom's first name)   (Bride's first name)

to be your wedded wife; promising to keep,
cherish, and protect her, and be her faith-

ful and true husband so long as you both
shall live?"

(Groom) "I do."

"_____, do you take _____
(Bride's first name)   (Groom's first name)

to be your wedded husband; promising to
love, honor, and obey him, and be his faithful and true wife so long as you both shall
live?"

(Bride) "I do."

"Who giveth this woman to be married to
this man?"

*Father or friend will answer: "I do"—and
join the right hand of the woman with the
right hand of the man. Then he shall retire to his appointed seat.*

*The man facing the woman and holding her
right hand, shall repeat after the minister:*

"I _____ take thee _____
(Groom's first name)   (Bride's first name)

to my wedded wife, to have and to hold,
from this day forward, for better for worse,
for richer for poorer, in sickness and in
health, to love and to cherish, till death us
do part, according to God's holy ordinance,
and thereto I give thee my troth."

*The woman facing the man and holding him
by the right hand, shall repeat after the minister:*

"I _____ take thee _____
(Bride's first name)   (Groom's first name)

to my wedded husband, to have and to hold, from this day forward, for better for worse, for richer for poorer, in sickness and in health, to love, to cherish, and to obey, till death us do part, according to God's holy ordinance, and thereto I give thee my troth."

"_____, what token do you give
(Groom's first name)

in acknowledgment of these vows?"

(Groom) "This ring." *Ring is handed to minister by best man.*

Handing the ring to the groom, the minister shall instruct him to place it on the ring finger of his bride's left hand. Then shall the minister say:

"This ring is of gold, and is precious; so let your love be your most cherished earthly possession."

"And _____, what token do you
(Bride's first name)

give in acknowledgment of your vows?"

(Bride) "This ring." *Ring is handed to minister by maid of honor. Handing the ring to the bride, the minister shall instruct her to place it on the ring finger of her groom's left hand. Then shall the minister say:*

"This ring is (these rings are) a perfect and unbroken circle, the symbol of eternity. So may your love be to all eternity.

"With these emblems of purity and endless devotion, showing how lasting and imperishable is the faith now mutually pledged, you do each the other wed and these marriage vows you do here and now forever seal.

"Let us pray."

Then joining their right hands and placing his right hand upon theirs, the minister shall say:

"Inasmuch as you have thus consented in holy wedlock, and have pledged the same before God and these friends, and have acknowledged your vows with the token of these rings, I, by virtue of the authority that is vested in me as a minister of the Word of God, and by the laws of this commonwealth pronounce you husband and wife, united in the pure and holy bonds of wedlock. Those whom God hath joined together, let no man put asunder."

The embrace and kiss may follow.

The benediction, followed by introduction of Mr. and Mrs. John Doe!

A SHORTER WEDDING CEREMONY

(Does not contain exchange of vows)

"And the Lord God said, It is not good that the man should be alone; I will make him an help meet for him. Therefore shall a man leave his father and his mother, and shall cleave unto his wife: and they shall be one flesh."

"Whoso findeth a wife findeth a good thing, and obtaineth favour of the Lord."

"Who can find a virtuous woman? for her price is far above rubies. The heart of her husband doth safely trust in her, so that he shall have no need of spoil. She will do him good and not evil all the days of her life."

"Marriage has always been a joyous occasion, gladdened by the presence and blessing of the Lord Jesus, and crowned with honor and sacred dignity by God Himself. Because God meant that it should bring blessing and happiness to your lives, let us invoke His Presence upon you as you pledge yourselves, each to the other, making your covenant and taking your vows before Him and this company.

"Let us pray." *Brief invocation.*

Then shall the minister say: "Who giveth

_____ to be married to _____
(Bride's full name)   (Groom's

_____?"
full name)

The bride's father shall say: "I do." (*Or he may say:* "Her mother and I.")

He will then be seated.

The minister shall say: "_____, do
(Groom's first name)

you take _____ to your wedded
(Bride's first name)

wife? Do you covenant to love, honor, and keep her; to cherish and comfort her; taking her for richer for poorer, for better for worse, in sickness and in health; to have and to hold from this time forth, cleaving to her alone till death do you part?"

The response: "I do."

Then shall the minister say: "_____,
(Bride's first name)

do you take _____ to your wedded
(Groom's first name)

husband? Do you covenant to love, honor, and obey him; cherish and comfort him; taking him for richer for poorer, for better for worse, in sickness and in health; to have and to hold from this time forth, cleaving to him alone till death do you part?"

The response: "I do."

The minister shall ask: "What token of the sincerity of this covenant do you give?"

The best man shall hand the ring to the groom, who will hand it to the minister.

The groom shall say: "This ring."

Then shall the minister say: "_____,
(Bride's first name)

do you in evidence of your love and sincerity accept this ring?"

The response: "I do."

The minister shall say: "This ring is a perfect circle of precious metal. The circle is a symbol of completeness and an emblem of eternity. The precious metal is that which has been tested and proved true. It is a fitting emblem of your love for each other and of your faith in each other. In the test of time, like gold in the fire, may your love and faith prove true and endure until death do you part."

Giving the ring to the groom, the minister shall say:

"Place this ring on the ring finger of _____
(Bride's

_____ left hand and repeat these words:
first name)

'With this ring I thee wed, and with all my heart's faithful affections I thee endow.'"

(For a double ring ceremony the above will be followed, beginning with the question:

"What token of the sincerity of this covenant do you give?" The maid of honor will hand the ring to the bride, and she will say: "This ring," etc.)

Then shall the minister unite the right hands of the bride and groom, and say:

"Inasmuch as you have mutually assumed this wedding covenant as a sacred vow taken before God and this company, by the authority conferred upon me as a minister of the Gospel, I do now pronounce you husband and wife in the name of the Father, and of the Son, and of the Holy Ghost. Those whom

God hath joined together let not man put asunder.

"Let us pray." *The bride and groom should kneel for this prayer of blessing, after which the minister may assist them to rise. The embrace and kiss may follow.*

Then shall the minister say: (Mr. and Mrs. _____) May the Lord bless thee and keep thee. May the Lord make His face to shine upon thee and be gracious unto thee. May the Lord lift up His countenance upon thee and give thee peace. Amen."

Then shall follow the recessional.

THE FUNERAL

INTRODUCTION

No demand upon a pastor is as urgent as the call of sorrow in the hour of bereavement and death. Never do his people need him as greatly or lean upon him so heavily. Nor does the door ever swing so widely to admit him into their hearts' affection and lasting memory as when he comes to bear them up in love and comfort. Most pastors know when their members may be sick unto death, and generally are near to comfort those to whom the shock is greatest. But should he, for one reason or another, not be present at the moment, he will go to the sorrowing ones as quickly as possible after the word reaches him and he will minister to them all that his human abilities and divine enablings will permit.

At a convenient moment, while meticulously avoiding the offering of his service, he should ascertain the wishes of the family concerning funeral arrangements. These plans should be followed as closely as possible, though he may tactfully suggest helpful changes. People of his congregation should be made aware of the death that they may offer Christian consolation, perform some thoughtful ministry, and attend the funeral service.

The funeral director generally contacts the minister to determine that all is in order, and that plans for the service are fully understood by both. It is not his prerogative to alter the plans or direct the conducting of the service. The pastor is responsible in this, and will kindly inform the director how the service is to proceed. If the assistance of another minister or the participation of an organization is to be included, such arrangements as are necessary shall be carefully made with them.

The pastor's attire will be appropriate, his decorum dignified. He may feel free to speak of the deceased's life and relationship to the church and community if circumstances seem to warrant it. No exaggerated eulogies are necessary. The message should be simple and brief, containing solace for the sorrowing, salvation for the sinner, and a glorious hope for all in Christ. A deliberate play upon emotions is unpardonable. Doctrinal dissertations and any other devices which might mar the Spirit's opportunity of moving souls to Christ should be avoided.

At the grave be brief especially if the weather is inclement. If possible avoid involvement with other organizations in rituals at the grave. After the benediction take time to clasp the hand of each mourner and speak warm words of comfort and encouragement. Promise a visit to the home within a day or two, and be sure the promise is kept.

If the deceased is a member or adherent of the church, a suitable word in the church bulletin will be appreciated by the bereaved. Often a favorite hymn of the deceased, sung at a Sunday service following the funeral, serves to cement the bonds of Christian sympathy and love between the church family and the sorrowing. An honorarium received for a funeral service should be acknowledged by a gracious letter of thanks and appreciation for the thoughtfulness. Some pastors feel that such an honorarium from members or regular attendants of the church should be returned with the letter. This should be determined by local conditions and personal conviction.

THE FUNERAL SERVICE

The service must not lack comfort and hope though it has order and dignity. The following is a suggested order which may be a helpful guide. Items inserted in parentheses may be omitted or included as the occasion may require.

Suggested Service	*Alternate Service*
Prelude	Prelude
Opening Scripture Sentence	Opening Scripture Sentence
Invocation	Invocation or Lord's Prayer
(Special music)	Obituary (if necessary)
(Obituary)	
Scripture	Scripture Reading
Prayer	Special Music
*(Special music)	Brief Message
Sermon	Pastoral Prayer
Prayer	Special Music
Postlude	Benediction
	Postlude

* NOTE: If only one musical selection is being used, this is perhaps the best time for it.

At the grave:

Committal Service

Benediction

Opening Scripture Sentence: Give thought and care to your choice so that it may be appropriate to the needs of the bereaved. It may be well to use a theme for the Scriptures chosen for the whole service, such as: comfort, faith, hope, strength, heaven, etc. The references given here are but a few of the many which are appropriate.

"And he said, My presence shall go with thee, and I will give thee rest." Exodus 33:14

"Let me die the death of the righteous, and let my last end be like his!" Numbers 23:10b

"Know therefore that the Lord thy God, he is God, the faithful God, which keepeth covenant and mercy with them that love him and keep his commandments to a thousand generations." Deuteronomy 7: 9

"The eternal God is thy refuge, and underneath are the everlasting arms." Deuteronomy 33: 27a

"The Lord gave, and the Lord hath taken away; blessed be the name of the Lord. . . . Though he slay me, yet will I trust in him." Job 1:21b; 13:15a

"For I know that my redeemer liveth, and that he shall stand at the latter day upon the earth. . . . Whom I shall see for myself, and mine eyes shall behold, and not another." Job 19:25, 27a

"God is our refuge and strength, a very present help in trouble." Psalm 46:1

"The name of the Lord is a strong tower: the righteous runneth into it, and is safe." Proverbs 18:10

"Lord, thou hast been our dwelling place in all generations. Before the mountains were brought forth, or ever thou hadst formed the earth and the world, even from everlasting to everlasting, thou art God." Psalm 90:1, 2

"He that dwelleth in the secret place of the most High shall abide under the shadow of the Almighty. I will say of the Lord, He is my refuge and my fortress: my God; in him will I trust." Psalm 91:1, 2

"Behold, God is my salvation; I will trust, and not be afraid: for the Lord JEHOVAH is my strength and my song; he also is become my salvation." Isaiah 12:2

"Thou wilt keep him in perfect peace, whose mind is stayed on thee: because he trusteth in thee. Trust ye in the Lord for ever: for in the Lord JEHOVAH is everlasting strength." Isaiah 26:3, 4

"Thine eyes shall see the king in his beauty: they shall behold the land that is very far off." Isaiah 33:17

"He shall feed his flock like a shepherd: he shall gather the lambs with his arm, and carry them in his bosom." Isaiah 40:11

"Fear thou not; for I am with thee: be not

dismayed; for I am thy God: I will strengthen thee; yea, I will help thee; yea, I will uphold thee with the right hand of my righteousness." Isaiah 41:10

"When thou passest through the waters, I will be with thee; and through the rivers, they shall not overflow thee: when thou walkest through the fire, thou shalt not be burned; neither shall the flame kindle upon thee. For I am the Lord thy God, the Holy One of Israel, thy Saviour." Isaiah 43:2, 3a

"Jesus said unto her, I am the resurrection, and the life: he that believeth in me, though he were dead, yet shall he live: And whosoever liveth and believeth in me shall never die." John 11:25, 26

"Blessed be God, even the Father of our Lord Jesus Christ, the Father of mercies, and the God of all comfort; Who comforteth us in all our tribulation, that we may be able to comfort them which are in any trouble, by the comfort wherewith we ourselves are comforted of God." 2 Corinthians 1:3, 4

"I have fought a good fight, I have finished my course, I have kept the faith: Henceforth there is laid up for me a crown of righteousness, which the Lord, the righteous judge, shall give me at that day: and not to me only, but unto all them also that love his appearing." 2 Timothy 4:7, 8

Invocation: This will be a brief prayer with clear, natural, well modulated voice. It will invoke quietness of spirit, yieldedness of the heart to the wisdom of God, grace for the present hour, and a deep sense of God's presence and comfort in the service.

Special music: The minister is often asked to secure musicians for the service, or include a certain favorite hymn to be sung by a friend. Since music, especially the human voice, is often harder to bear than the bereaved realize, special selections should be kept at a minimum where it can be tactfully done. However, it is the family's prerogative to choose music, and the minister's restraint should be delicate. This does not mean to discredit the ministry of music, for it certainly has its place, but merely calls for caution that such a ministry shall be that of comfort. Many ministers, in the absence of vocal and instrumental music, choose to read the strengthening words of some stately hymn, or a poem of good taste and comfort.

Obituary: This feature of the service has all but disappeared. It formerly served as a general resumé and sometimes as a eulogy of the deceased. While it is the family's prerogative to choose whether there is to be an obituary, it is not wise to suggest one. If one is submitted by the family, it should be used, though it may be edited for the sake of clarity and accuracy.

Scripture: The scripture portion should be read slowly and distinctly. This is the longer of the portions to be read, and may be the foundation of the message. If some theme is being followed, as suggested earlier, this will be the

full development of that theme.   One or more
of the following may be used:

"The Lord is my light and my salvation;
whom shall I fear? the Lord is the strength
of my life; of whom shall I be afraid? . . .
One thing have I desired of the Lord, that
will I seek after; that I may dwell in the
house of the Lord all the days of my life, to
behold the beauty of the Lord, and to in-
quire in his temple.   For in the time of trouble he shall hide me in his pavilion: in the
secret of his tabernacle shall he hide me;
he shall set me up upon a rock.   And now
shall mine head be lifted up above mine enemies round about me: therefore will I offer
in his tabernacle sacrifices of joy; I will sing,
yea, I will sing praises unto the Lord. Hear,
O Lord, when I cry with my voice: have
mercy also upon me, and answer me.   When
thou saidst, Seek ye my face; my heart said
unto thee, Thy face, Lord, will I seek. . . .
Wait on the Lord: be of good courage, and
he shall strengthen thine heart: wait, I say,
on the Lord." Psalm 27:1, 4-8, 14

"He that walketh righteously, and speaketh uprightly; he that despiseth the gain of
oppressions, that shaketh his hands from
holding of bribes, that stoppeth his ears from
hearing of blood, and shutteth his eyes from
seeing evil; He shall dwell on high: his place

of defence shall be the munitions of the rocks: bread shall be given him; his waters shall be sure. Thine eyes shall see the king in his beauty: they shall behold the land that is very far off. . . . But there the glorious Lord will be unto us a place of broad rivers and streams; wherein shall go no galley with oars, neither shall gallant ship pass thereby. For the Lord is our judge, the Lord is our lawgiver, the Lord is our king; he will save us. . . . And the inhabitant shall not say, I am sick: the people that dwell therein shall be forgiven their iniquity." Isaiah 33:15-17, 21, 22, 24

"Hast thou not known? hast thou not heard, that the everlasting God, the Lord, the Creator of the ends of the earth, fainteth not, neither is weary? there is no searching of his understanding. He giveth power to the faint; and to them that have no might he increaseth strength. . . . But they that wait upon the Lord shall renew their strength; they shall mount up with wings as eagles; they shall run, and not be weary; and they shall walk, and not faint." Isaiah 40:28, 29, 31

"Now this I say, brethren, that flesh and blood cannot inherit the kingdom of God; neither doth corruption inherit incorruption. Behold, I shew you a mystery; We shall not all sleep, but we shall all be changed, In a moment, in the twinkling of an eye, at the last trump: for the trumpet shall sound, and the dead shall be raised incorruptible, and we shall be changed. For this corruptible must put on incorruption, and this mortal must put on immortality. So when this corruptible shall have put on incorruption, and this mortal shall have put on immortality, then shall be brought to pass the saying that is written, Death is swallowed up in victory. O death, where is thy sting? O grave, where is thy victory? The sting of death is sin; and the strength of sin is the law. But thanks be to God, which giveth us the victory through our Lord Jesus Christ. Therefore, my beloved brethren, be ye stedfast, unmoveable, always abounding in the work of the Lord, forasmuch as ye know that your labour is not in vain in the Lord." 1 Corinthians 15: 50-58

"But I would not have you to be ignorant, brethren, concerning them which are asleep, that ye sorrow not, even as others which have no hope. For if we believe that Jesus died and rose again, even so them also which sleep in Jesus will God bring with him. For this we say unto you by the word of the Lord, that we which are alive and remain unto the coming of the Lord shall not prevent them which are asleep. For the Lord himself shall descend from heaven with a shout, with the voice of the archangel, and with the trump of God: and the dead in Christ shall rise first:

Then we which are alive and remain shall be caught up together with them in the clouds, to meet the Lord in the air: and so shall we ever be with the Lord. Wherefore comfort one another with these words." 1 Thessalonians 4:13-18

FOR A CHILD OR YOUTH

"David therefore besought God for the child; and David fasted, and went in, and lay all night upon the earth. And the elders of his house arose, and went to him, to raise him up from the earth: but he would not, neither did he eat bread with them. And it came to pass on the seventh day, that the child died. And the servants of David feared to tell him that the child was dead: for they said, Behold, while the child was yet alive, we spake unto him, and he would not hearken unto our voice: how will he then vex himself, if we tell him that the child is dead? But when David saw that his servants whispered, David perceived that the child was dead: therefore David said unto his servants, Is the child dead? And they said, He is dead. Then David arose from the earth, and washed, and anointed himself, and changed his apparel, and came into the house of the Lord, and worshipped: then he came to his own house; and when he required, they set bread before him, and he did eat. Then said his servants unto him, What thing is this

that thou hast done? thou didst fast and weep
for the child, while it was alive; but when the
child was dead, thou didst rise and eat bread.
And he said, While the child was yet alive,
I fasted and wept: for I said, Who can tell
whether God will be gracious to me, that the
child may live? But now he is dead, wherefore should I fast? can I bring him back
again? I shall go to him, but he shall not
return to me." 2 Samuel 12:16-23

"The Lord is my shepherd; I shall not
want. He maketh me to lie down in green
pastures: he leadeth me beside the still waters. He restoreth my soul: he leadeth me in
the paths of righteousness for his name's sake.
Yea, though I walk through the valley of the
shadow of death, I will fear no evil: for thou
art with me; thy rod and thy staff they comfort me. Thou preparest a table before me
in the presence of mine enemies: thou anoint-
est my head with oil; my cup runneth over.
Surely goodness and mercy shall follow me
all the days of my life: and I will dwell in
the house of the Lord for ever." Psalm 23

"And they brought young children to him,
that he should touch them: and his disciples
rebuked those that brought them. But when
Jesus saw it, he was much displeased, and
said unto them, Suffer the little children to
come unto me, and forbid them not: for of
such is the kingdom of God. Verily I say
unto you, Whosoever shall not receive the

kingdom of God as a little child, he shall not enter therein. And he took them up in his arms, put his hands upon them, and blessed them." Mark 10:13-16

FOR A FAITHFUL ADULT

"Blessed is the man that walketh not in the counsel of the ungodly, nor standeth in the way of sinners, nor sitteth in the seat of the scornful. But his delight is in the law of the Lord; and in his law doth he meditate day and night. And he shall be like a tree planted by the rivers of water, that bringeth forth his fruit in his season; his leaf also shall not wither; and whatsoever he doeth shall prosper. The ungodly are not so: but are like the chaff which the wind driveth away. Therefore the ungodly shall not stand in the judgment, nor sinners in the congregation of the righteous. For the Lord knoweth the way of the righteous: but the way of the ungodly shall perish." Psalm 1

"Lord, who shall abide in thy tabernacle? who shall dwell in thy holy hill? He that walketh uprightly, and worketh righteousness, and speaketh the truth in his heart. He that backbiteth not with his tongue, nor doeth evil to his neighbour, nor taketh up a reproach against his neighbour. In whose eyes a vile person is contemned; but he honoureth them that fear the Lord. He that sweareth to his own hurt, and changeth not. He that put-

teth not out his money to usury, nor taketh
reward against the innocent. He that doeth
these things shall never be moved." Psalm 15

"Who can find a virtuous woman? for her
price is far above rubies. The heart of her
husband doth safely trust in her, so that he
shall have no need of spoil. She will do him
good and not evil all the days of her life.
. . . She stretcheth out her hand to the poor;
yea, she reacheth forth her hands to the
needy. . . . Strength and honour are her
clothing; and she shall rejoice in time to
come. She openeth her mouth with wisdom;
and in her tongue is the law of kindness. She
looketh well to the ways of her household,
and eateth not the bread of idleness. Her
children arise up, and call her blessed; her
husband also, and he praiseth her. Many
daughters have done virtuously, but thou
excellest them all. Favour is deceitful, and
beauty is vain: but a woman that feareth the
Lord, she shall be praised. Give her of the
fruit of her hands; and let her own works
praise her in the gates." Proverbs 31:10-12,
20, 25-31

"Let not your heart be troubled: ye believe
in God, believe also in me. In my Father's
house are many mansions: if it were not so,
I would have told you. I go to prepare a
place for you. And if I go and prepare a
place for you, I will come again, and receive
you unto myself; that where I am, there ye

may be also. And whither I go ye know, and
the way ye know. Thomas saith unto him,
Lord, we know not whither thou goest; and
how can we know the way? Jesus saith unto
him, I am the way, the truth, and the life:
no man cometh unto the Father, but by me.
. . . Peace I leave with you, my peace I give
unto you: not as the world giveth, give I
unto you. Let not your heart be troubled,
neither let it be afraid." John 14:1-6, 27

"Blessed be the God and Father of our
Lord Jesus Christ, which according to his
abundant mercy hath begotten us again unto
a lively hope by the resurrection of Jesus
Christ from the dead, To an inheritance incorruptible, and undefiled, and that fadeth
not away, reserved in heaven for you, Who
are kept by the power of God through faith
unto salvation ready to be revealed in the
last time. Wherein ye greatly rejoice, though
now for a season, if need be, ye are in heavi-
ness through manifold temptations: That the
trial of your faith, being much more precious
than of gold that perisheth, though it be
tried with fire, might be found unto praise
and honour and glory at the appearing of
Jesus Christ: Whom having not seen, ye love;
in whom, though now ye see him not, yet believing, ye rejoice with joy unspeakable and
full of glory: Receiving the end of your faith,
even the salvation of your souls." 1 Peter
1:3-9

FOR AN ELDERLY PERSON

"Lord, thou hast been our dwelling place in all generations. Before the mountains were brought forth, or ever thou hadst formed the earth and the world, even from everlasting to everlasting, thou art God. Thou turnest man to destruction; and sayest, Return, ye children of men. For a thousand years in thy sight are but as yesterday when it is past, and as a watch in the night. Thou carriest them away as with a flood; they are as a sleep: in the morning they are like grass which groweth up. In the morning it flourisheth, and groweth up; in the evening it is cut down, and withereth. . . . For all our days are passed away in thy wrath: we spend our years as a tale that is told. The days of our years are threescore years and ten; and if by reason of strength they be fourscore years, yet is their strength labour and sorrow; for it is soon cut off, and we fly away. . . . So teach us to number our days, that we may apply our hearts unto wisdom." Psalm 90: 1-6, 9, 10, 12

"He that dwelleth in the secret place of the Most High shall abide under the shadow of the Almighty. I will say of the Lord, He is my refuge and my fortress: my God; in him will I trust. Surely he shall deliver thee from the snare of the fowler, and from the noisome pestilence. He shall cover thee with his feathers, and under his wings shalt thou trust: his truth shall be thy shield and buckler." Psalm 91:1-4

"And I saw a new heaven and a new earth: for the first heaven and the first earth were passed away; and there was no more sea. And I John saw the holy city, new Jerusalem, coming down from God out of heaven, prepared as a bride adorned for her husband. And I heard a great voice out of heaven saying, Behold, the tabernacle of God is with men, and he will dwell with them, and they shall be his people, and God himself shall be with them, and be their God. And God shall wipe away all tears from their eyes; and there shall be no more death, neither sorrow, nor crying, neither shall there be any more pain: for the former things are passed away. And he that sat upon the throne said, Behold, I make all things new. And he said unto me, Write: for these words are true and faithful. And he said unto me, It is done. I am Alpha and Omega, the beginning and the end. I will give unto him that is athirst of the fountain of the water of life freely. He that overcometh shall inherit all things; and I will be his God, and he shall be my son." Revelation 21:1-7

"And he shewed me a pure river of water of life, clear as crystal, proceeding out of the throne of God and of the Lamb. In the midst of the street of it, and on either side of the river, was there the tree of life, which bare twelve manner of fruits, and yielded her fruit every month: and the leaves of the tree were for the healing of the nations. And there shall be no more curse: but the throne of God and of the Lamb shall be in it; and his servants shall serve him: And they shall see his face; and his name shall be in their foreheads. And there shall be no night there; and they need no candle, neither light of the sun; for the Lord God giveth them light: and they shall reign for ever and ever." Revelation 22:1-5

Prayer: Make the prayer a simple, heart-felt petition in behalf of those who sorrow. If they are members of the church or well-known friends, it is sometimes well to use their names and pray for the principal mourners individually. But if a petition is offered that any who know not Christ may be led to prepare for meeting God, such petition should be impersonal, no identification is permissible.

Sermon: The Scriptures abound with an inexhaustible supply of texts for this ministry. The message itself will always be brief, simple, and comforting, never delivered in harsh or loud tones, always directed "to the living and not to the dead." Let there be abundant expressions of comfort. The admonition to "comfort ye, comfort ye my people" would certainly find propitious fulfillment in the message to the bereaved. Upon occasions where the deceased is known to be a child of God, there will be no lack of sources to which to direct the sorrowing for solace, comfort and hope.

The message will also hold forth the way of salvation to all who hear. A message that automatically preaches everyone into heaven is a disgrace to the ministry, a discredit to the intelligence of the company present, and a serious deviation from the truth of Scripture. On the other hand, be content to leave with God the final destiny of one about whose spiritual standing there may be reason to doubt. The Judge of all the earth will do right. The minister will not have to express his judgment. Occasionally the minister is asked to give an invitation to a public profession of faith following his message. He will explain this request, and extend the invitation as simply and seemly as possible. Certainly it does not seem wise to ask people to move forward around the casket, but rather it would suffice to raise a hand, or stand to the feet. He may wisely add that he wishes to speak with these persons at his earliest convenience, to confirm their decision. But whether a public profession is included or not, the message should point up the need for a personal experience of faith.

Prayer: This will be brief, asking that the sorrowing might be enabled to direct their hearts and hopes to the Word just set before them, finding its strength and solace for their need now and in days to come.

NOTE: If the burial will be at some distant place where most of those now present will not attend the committal service, the minister here will do well to read a brief appropriate passage selected from the committal liturgy and then conclude with one of the following sentences as is appropriate: (For a Christian) "We now commit the body of our departed brother (sister) to those who will convey it to another community there to be laid to rest until the soon coming of our Lord and the resurrection of the dead in Christ." (For a non-Christian) "We now commit the body of our departed friend to those who will convey it to another community there to be laid to rest."

Then will follow a benediction and the funeral director will assume charge. If there is to be a viewing of the body he will direct. Generally, after viewing the body, the people leave the building and the minister does not need to accompany the body to the funeral car.

If the burial will be local and attended by those now present, the prayer should end with a benediction and the funeral director will then take charge. If there is to be a final viewing of the body he will direct this, as well as the departure from the building to the funeral procession. The minister waits in the place indicated until the casket is in readiness to be taken to the funeral car. He with the director will precede the pallbearers and casket to the car. From thence he will go to the car which is to convey him to the cemetery.

Committal Service: At the cemetery, the minister, accompanied by the funeral director, will proceed slowly ahead of the casket to the grave, where he will stand at the end or to the rear until all the persons are assembled. Upon a signal from the director that all is in readiness, he may begin. A brief passage of Scripture may be read, sometimes a familiar hymn of consolation is sung, and then the committal is made followed by the benediction.

Scripture passages and a committal may be selected from the following:

FOR A BELIEVER

1 Thessalonians 4:13-18 or

1 Corinthians 15:51-58

"Friends, we gather here to commit to this resting place the body of our beloved brother (sister) whose spirit is already with the Lord. While this spot of earth will hold the form of one whose memory we shall always treasure, we look not here in sorrow as those who have no hope. We believe that to be absent from the body is to be present with the Lord, and that to die is gain. We therefore commit his (her) body to the ground in the renewed and fresh hope of the soon coming of Christ, at whose appearing the dead in Christ shall rise and we which are alive and remain, shall be caught up together with them to meet the Lord in the air. And thus shall we ever be with the Lord. Wherefore, we comfort one another with these words."

OR,

"Hear the comforting words of Scripture: 'The Lord gave, and the Lord hath taken away; blessed be the name of the Lord.' 'Let not your heart be troubled, neither let it be afraid.'

"We have gathered here, friends, to commit to this resting place the body of our beloved brother (sister):

Cherishing memories that are forever sacred;
Sustained by a faith that is stronger than
       death;
And comforted by the hope of a life that shall
       endless be,
We commit to the earth all that is mortal of
       this, our friend.
As we have borne the image of the earthly,
So shall we bear the image of the heavenly."

OR,

" 'The Lord is my light and my salvation; whom shall I fear? the Lord is the strength of my life; of whom shall I be afraid? . . . One thing have I desired of the Lord, that will I seek after; that I may dwell in the house of the Lord all the days of my life, to behold the beauty of the Lord, and to enquire in his temple.'

"Some of us have shared through these passing years a wonderful companionship and fellowship with our beloved and faithful brother (sister). Many blessed and hallowed memories come to us in these moments which we shall always cherish. His (her) faithfulness, friendliness, and consecrated life will continue their radiance and testimony in our lives, our church, and our community. In the name of Jesus Christ,

whom he (she) loved and served, we commit his (her) body to this resting place,
knowing that his (her) spirit is with the Lord
in His house of many mansions. And in so
doing, we rest our hearts in fresh confidence
upon the sure and certain hope of the resurrection unto life eternal through Jesus Christ
our Lord."

OR,

"Forasmuch as it hath pleased Almighty
God in His great mercy to take unto Himself the soul of our dear brother (sister) here
departed: we therefore commit his (her)
body to the ground; earth to earth, ashes to
ashes, dust to dust; in the sure and certain
hope of the resurrection to life eternal
through our Lord Jesus Christ; who shall
change our corruptible body, that it may be
like unto His glorious body, according to the
working of His mighty power whereby He is
able to subdue all things unto Himself.
Amen."

FOR A CHILD

Isaiah 40:11 or Mark 10:13-16

" 'He took the children in His arms and
blessed them.' Let us take this scene from
the earthly life of our Lord and transform it
into a heavenly vision. Again His arms have
opened to a little child whom He has clasped
to His bosom in tenderest love. He has instructed us to suffer the little children to

4

come unto Him, and to forbid them not. The going of this one so dear to our hearts has actually brought heaven nearer to our souls."

OR,

"Of such is the kingdom of heaven. To-day we feel that heaven is more real than ever, and that we have held eternity in our arms when we have held this little one. Let us heed the word of Jesus that instructs us to become as little children that we too might enter the Kingdom of Heaven. Would that all were as sure as their soul's entrance into the Kingdom, as we are of this little one's welcome there. Being comforted then by this truth, we commit his (her) little body to this place of rest. We here renew our determination to give heed to our own soul's need that we too may inherit eternal life through Jesus Christ our Lord."

OR,

" 'Suffer the little children to come unto me and forbid them not, for of such is the Kingdom of God.' 'The Eternal God is thy refuge and underneath are the everlasting arms.' Forasmuch as it hath pleased the Heavenly Father and Shepherd of the lambs to take unto His heavenly fold the soul of this child, we therefore commit his (her) body to the ground. 'And they shall be mine, saith the Lord of Hosts, in that day when I make up my jewels.' 'They shall hunger no more,

neither shall the sun light on them, nor any
heat. For the Lamb which is in the midst
of the throne shall feed them, and shall lead
them unto living fountains of waters; and
God shall wipe away all tears from their
eyes.'"

FOR A NON-CHRISTIAN

*Portions from Psalm 46, 90, 91, 103, John 14
or John 11:25-36*

"It is here that we pay the last respect of
the living to the dead. Man that is born
of woman hath but a short time to live, and
is full of trouble. We brought nothing into
this world and it is certain that we can carry
nothing out. In the midst of life we are in
the midst of death. And from whom can we
seek for help, but from the Lord, who is
justly displeased with our sins? This is the
end of all the living; may the living lay it to
heart. There is no work, nor knowledge, nor
device, nor wisdom in the grave to which
we go. Knowing that it is appointed unto
man once to die and after this the judgment,
let us here purpose to seek the Lord with all
our hearts and respond to the opportunities
of salvation extended us through His grace.
The Scripture says it is God's goodness that
leads us to repentance. And repentance leads
us to His greatest gift, the gift of eternal life
through the Lord Jesus Christ. May each
gift of God's goodness remind us of His love

toward us in Christ. We commit now the body of this loved one to this resting place; the spirit we leave with God, for we know the Judge of all the earth will do right."

OR,

"Jesus said, 'Verily, verily I say unto you, He that heareth my word, and believeth on him that sent me, hath everlasting life, and shall not come into condemnation; but is passed from death unto life. . . . Marvel not at this: for the hour is coming, in the which all that are in the graves shall hear his voice, And shall come forth; they that have done good, unto the resurrection of life; and they that have done evil, unto the resurrection of damnation.' Forasmuch as it hath pleased Almighty God to take from this world the soul of our departed friend, we commit his (her) body to the ground to await the resurrection as foretold by Jesus Christ."

Benediction: Proceed from the committal into the benediction, praying once more for the comfort of the sorrowing, and for their adjustment and wisdom for the days that lie ahead. At his discretion, the minister may choose to conclude with a familiar benediction from Scripture:

"The Lord bless thee, and keep thee: The Lord make his face shine upon thee, and be gracious unto thee: The Lord lift up his countenance upon thee, and give thee peace." Numbers 6:24-26

"And the peace of God, which passeth all understanding, . . . keep your hearts and minds through Christ Jesus." Philippians 4:7

"Now our Lord Jesus Christ himself, and God, even our Father, which hath loved us, and hath given us everlasting consolation and good hope through grace, Comfort your hearts, and stablish you in every good word and work." 2 Thessalonians 2:16, 17

"Now the God of peace, that brought again from the dead our Lord Jesus, that great shepherd of the sheep, through the blood of the everlasting covenant, Make you perfect in every good work to do his will, working in you that which is wellpleasing in his sight, through Jesus Christ; to whom be glory for ever and ever. Amen." Hebrews 13:20, 21

The grave-side service is frequently the most difficult for the mourners. It is sometimes terrifying to them to think of leaving their loved one there to be buried in the ground, to be seen no more. The minister, therefore, as soon as he concludes the service, may step to the side of the principal mourners to give his personal word of encouragement to them. He may linger with them a moment to be of any assistance that he can, should they be overcome by emotion. At the conclusion of the service, there is frequently an opportune moment to speak quietly with some individual about his spiritual needs.

BAPTISM

INTRODUCTION

Baptism is one of the two ordinances enjoined upon believers by the Lord Jesus. Reaction to certain abuses of this ordinance, particularly doctrinal abuses, has led many to treat it as unimportant and optional to the Christian life. Such a position is as extreme as the abuse against which it protests. Universal Christian testimony assures us that its participants have found baptism to be a significant spiritual experience. Therefore, let the Lord's servant set forth the scriptural purpose of baptism in such a way as to encourage believers to enter in.

There are some details which the minister must cover to assure proper spiritual participation of the candidate, as well as the smooth function of the administration of the ordinance.

a. He will want to be assured of the genuineness of the candidate's regeneration. People frequently present themselves for baptism simply because some relative or friend is doing so, or because they have a mental sense of duty rather than a spiritual sense of obedience and testimony.

b. A careful, though not lengthy, review of the meaning and purpose of the ordinance with each candidate is in order.

c. Instruction as to the proper mode of dress, change of clothing, etc., is of real help to the candidate. The minister will also explain just what is to be done during the administration of the ordinance so there will be neither fear nor embarrassment.

Thus the necessary dignity of the service is maintained. The following, or similar instructions should be given: As instructed by the minister, the candidate shall come into the water and face the congregation. As the words of the baptismal formula are spoken, the candidate shall clasp the minister's wrist with both of his hands. The minister holding a folded handkerchief over the candidate's nose and mouth, and placing his other hand back of the candidate's shoulders, will lower him backward into the water. The minister will assist as he rises from the water.

d. Definite arrangements should be made for proper dressing rooms, and for someone to aid the candidates going into and coming out of the water. Towels should be provided for those who may forget their own. The temperature of the water ought to be regulated to the season of the year if the ordinance is to be performed in the church baptistry.

THE SERVICE

Attention should be given to the planning of this service, whether it be included in a regular church service, or planned and conducted as a separate service. Many churches emphasize it as part of a regular evening service as a means of publicity. But at whatever time or place the ordinance may be administered, its sacredness calls for careful planning and dignified conduct, if its spiritual impact is to be felt.

Since the ordinance is most commonly included as a part of a regular service, the following is a suggested order:

1. Appropriate hymn, while the minister takes his place in the water.

2. Read or quote from memory one or more of these or other passages of Scripture:

Mat. 3: 13-17   Acts 8: 35-39
Mat. 28: 16-20   Rom. 6: 1-5
Mark 16: 14-18   Col. 2: 12-14

3. Brief remarks.

4. Address to each candidate:

"Do you have a clear witness from God that you are His child through faith in the Lord Jesus Christ as your personal Saviour?"

The response—"I do."

"Is it your earnest desire to follow Christ in death to self and to walk with Him in newness of life, of which life this ordinance is a symbol?"

The response—"It is."

(Note: After questioning the candidate, opportunity may be given for personal testimony, if desired.)

"_____, upon your confession of faith in the Lord Jesus Christ as your personal Saviour, and by this step of obedience to Him in this ordinance, expressing your desire to follow Him in death to self and to walk with Him in newness of life, I baptize you in the name of the Father, and of the Son, and of the Holy Ghost. Amen." (Here the candidate is immersed as directed in the preceding paragraphs.)

5. A verse of song or a chorus may be sung or played during the interval between candidates, if desired.

Upon occasions where baptism is administered at an outdoor service, the above order may be lengthened. The brief remarks may be extended, congregational singing or special music added, and testimonies by the candidates included.

Properly prepared certificates should be presented to the candidates at the close of the service, or very soon thereafter. The church records should also bear entry of the names and date of the event.

EQUIPMENT

Waterproof equipment is available for use by ministers, which requires but a minimum of robing and disrobing. Whatever he chooses to wear, a dark suit, or white shirt and trousers, let him allow ample time in the planning of the service for his own dressing and returning to the platform if such is expected. Robes and gowns are likewise available for the candidates to wear, both white and black. (Some churches make their own.) If ordinary dress is worn, let it be clean and of sufficient modesty to cover the body when wet and clinging.

COMMUNION

INTRODUCTION

The most blessed and sacred bond between the body of believers and their risen Lord, and between one another, is experienced in the sacrament of the Communion. It is an experience of the heart and mind merging in singleness of de-

votion to the Person and work of the Lord Jesus
Christ. It is a moment of high spiritual experience, and we should never be content to let it be
anything less. No other service so reflects the
vital elements of Christian experience and faith
as this. But, sadly enough, no other service seems
to have become so stifled with meaningless for-
mality and lifeless ritual. Let the man of God
purpose to so understand its truth, and so direct
its observance, as to bring its holy significance
within the experience of each participant, every
time it is observed.

Preparation of the table and the elements are
the concern of the minister. He will see that
these matters are in the hands of responsible persons. Clean linens for the table, clean vessels
for the emblems, and clean men for the service
are indispensable. Those who assist at the table
should be well informed as to what is expected
of them, and how the service is to proceed.

The place to be given to Communion in a regular worship service is important. Three things
will guide in this: Let it never be observed as an
appendage to a service; let it never be unrelated
to the theme of the service; and let it never be
observed with haste. Its holy character and spiritual content demand for Communion the climac-
tic point in the worship service. When it is to be
observed let all parts of the service contribute to
its meaning, and prepare for its ministry.

In some areas the custom prevails to dismiss
unbelievers and those who do not wish to remain,
before Communion is observed. This appears to
be without scriptural warrant, and certainly its
propriety is questioned. Let the minister most
certainly make it clear in a gracious manner that
the Lord's table is only for the Lord's people,
born again and living a holy life. But beyond

that he is not called to go. "Let a man examine himself."

SIMULTANEOUS COMMUNION

The form for simultaneous Communion is most commonly used. It provides that communicants retain the bread when they are served, and all partake together at a given signal; likewise the cup.

The minister shall give the invitation to partake, emphasizing its seriousness and significance.

The elders make an orderly and dignified approach to the table. (They may be instructed to remove the linens, if desired.)

Minister quotes from memory: "I have received of the Lord that which also I delivered unto you, That the Lord Jesus the same night in which he was betrayed took bread: And when he had given thanks." 1 Corinthians 11:23-24.

Prayer of thanks for the bread. (One of the elders may offer this prayer.)

Minister quotes: "When he had given thanks, he break it, and said, Take, eat: this is my body, which is broken for you; this do in remembrance of me." He will request the congregation to retain the bread in their hand until all have been served. He then hands the bread to the elders and takes his seat as they distribute it.

Music may be played softly, or the congregation may sing or there may be silent prayer during the distribution.

Upon their return to the table, the minister takes the bread from the elders and serves them, lastly taking a portion for himself. The elders are seated and the minister, holding the bread, may quote Scripture or speak a sentence extemporaneously. His words should be calculated to fix the heart on Jesus Christ the Lord in devotion, worship and adoration.

NOTE: It is also appropriate as a variation to have the prayer of thanks after all have been served—so that partaking immediately follows the prayer.

The bread is partaken of simultaneously, followed by a brief silence for meditation.

Minister quotes: "After the same manner also he took the cup." Elders stand. Prayer of thanks for the cup. (One of the elders may be asked to offer this prayer.)

Minister quotes: "He took the cup, when he had supped, saying, This cup is the new testament in my blood; this do ye, as oft as ye drink it, in remembrance of me. For as often as ye eat this bread, and drink this cup, ye do shew the Lord's death till he come." He will request the congregation to retain the cup in hand until all have been served. The trays are then handed to the elders for distribution, and he is seated. (Again music may be played softly, the congregation may sing, or there may be silent prayer during the distribution.)

Upon their return to the table, the minister takes the trays from the elders and serves them, lastly taking a cup himself. The elders are seated, and the minister, holding the cup, may pray, quote Scripture, or speak extemporaneously in like manner as he did with the bread.

(See Note above.)

The cup is taken simultaneously, followed by a brief silence for meditation. Then shall the minister offer prayer.

(If receptacles are provided in the pews for the glasses they may be left there. Otherwise the elders return and collect them.)

Benevolent Offering. (If it is the custom of the church, ushers should be instructed in advance to be ready.)

Hymn.

Benediction.

COMMUNION AT THE ALTAR

The practice of serving the emblems to communicants while they kneel at the altar is regularly followed in many churches. If the physical properties permit a large enough altar to accommodate a number of persons at a time, and if the congregation is not so large as to require too many servings, this mode of communing has much to commend it. The service would be much the same as above. The minister would invite believers to come forward from the first few rows until the altar was filled. These would first be served the bread, then the cup. They would then retire to their seats and others come in like manner until all had been served. Aged and infirm persons could be instructed to be seated on the front pew to be served if they could not kneel. This type of service would require a longer period of time than the other type where the emblems are distributed. However, the important consideration is not the time element but rather the spiritual benefit derived.

VARIATIONS

The general service already outlined may be followed, but with these changes: Read or quote appropriate Scriptures, before distribution of the bread and cup. Then the distribution may be conducted in entire silence, or with singing, or with testimony.

OR,

One group of elders may distribute the bread and another the cup, following as close to one another as is orderly and dignified. Then the partaking may be simultaneous.

OR,

The communicants may serve each other, adding a closer touch of fellowship at the table. The elder hands the emblems to the second person in the row, who then serves the first person and passes the plate or tray on to the third person. Then the third person serves the second, and likewise passes the emblems on, until all serve each other. The elder will receive the emblems at the end of the pew and serve the last person in the row. This type of observance requires clear and simple explanation to operate smoothly.

OR,

The entire worship service may be conducted from the table, no sermon, as such, being given. Minute preparation is absolutely necessary lest the service seem to lack in its essential elements. But its apparent deviation from accustomed routine need not rob the service of freshness and inspiration.

DEDICATION OF CHILDREN

INTRODUCTION

There appears to be wide latitude in the interpretation of the meaning and practice of dedicating children to God. As a rite, it may be without scriptural commandment but not without scriptural example. Certainly one does not insist that parents were "dedicating" their children when they brought them to Christ to be blessed by Him. But God's peculiar claim upon the first-born Israelites, the explicit record of Hannah with Samuel, and the presentation of Christ in the Temple are not without significance.

Who may dedicate a child to God? Some answer that it makes no difference as to the spiritual status of the parents. Others disagree, claiming that one of the parents must be a Christian before it is appropriate. And yet others hold that both parents must be Christians if the act is to have proper significance. There appears to be scarcely any common ground between these views upon which a compromise can be effected. The more one attaches spiritual significance to the rite, the more inclined he is to raise the qualifications for participation.

It is not the purpose of this Handbook to present arguments. The following form is presented containing the term: "Christian parents," and may be modified according to the user's own wisdom.

The minister, upon learning of the parents' desire to dedicate their child, will visit them in their home to discuss with them the service and its significance. The door is usually wide open for his approach to their personal spiritual needs. If they were prompted by sentiment rather than devotion, to dedicate their child, he can tactfully show them the difference and draw them to the spiritual purpose. Should they be unbelievers, the minister has an unparalleled opportunity to invite them to come to God themselves as they bring the child. He will explain the manner in which the service is conducted and the time it will be scheduled in the worship hour. He will also obtain the correctly spelled name of the child and his parents, and the correct birth date. This information will later be entered in the church records, and on a certificate which the minister will give the parents following the service.

The dedication ceremony should be included early in the program of worship, before the child becomes restless.

THE DEDICATION CEREMONY

The pianist or organist may play softly, or the congregation may sing some appropriate hymn, such as "Jewels" or "I Think When I Read That Sweet Story." An appointed usher may bring the parents forward with their child to stand before the minister, the father holding the child in his arms if an infant.

The minister may read one or more of the following, or other Scriptures:

"Hear, O Israel: The Lord our God is one Lord: And thou shalt love the Lord thy God with all thine heart, and with all thy soul, and with all thy might. And these words, which I command thee this day, shall be in thine heart; And thou shalt teach them diligently unto thy children, and shalt talk of them when thou sittest in thine house, and when thou walkest by the way, and when thou liest down, and when thou risest up." Deuteronomy 6:4-7

OR,

"But the mercy of the Lord is from everlasting to everlasting upon them that fear him, and his righteousness unto children's children; To such as keep his covenant, and to those that remember his commandments to do them." Psalm 103:17, 18

OR,

"And Jesus called a little child unto him, and set him in the midst of them, And said, Verily I say unto you, Except ye be converted, and become as little children, ye shall not enter into the kingdom of heaven. Whosoever therefore shall humble himself as this little child, the same is greatest in the kingdom of heaven. And whoso shall receive one such little child in my name receiveth me. But whoso shall offend one of these little ones which believe in me, it were better for him that a millstone were hanged about his neck, and that he were drowned in the depth of the sea." Matthew 18:2-6

Then shall the minister offer prayer; thankfulness for Christian parents, invoking God's blessing upon parents and child.

Address to parents: "Christian parents, in presenting your child to the Lord, you enter into a solemn relationship with God who keepeth covenant to a thousand generations.

5

Throughout the ages godly parents have presented their children to God in dedication. You follow a noble heritage.

"Believing that this child is a gift from God, and that He shall hold you accountable for him, (her) do you now solemnly confess that it is your purpose to dedicate him (her) to the Lord and to His service? Will you pray with him, (her) and for him, (her) instruct him (her) faithfully in the doctrines of the Christian religion; teach him, (her) to read the Word of God, to pray, and to lead a holy life; take him (her) faithfully to the House of God to attend its services; and do all that in you lies to bring him (her) to the knowledge of Jesus Christ as Saviour and Lord?"

The response—"I will."

The Dedication. *The minister, announcing the name of the child, and taking the child in his arms or laying his hand upon its head, shall say:*

"   (John Doe)   , I now dedicate thee to God in the name of the Father, and of the Son, and of the Holy Ghost. May thy young life be nurtured and matured under the gracious influence of the Holy Spirit. May God early call thee into His Kingdom, and into His service, using thee to advance His glory and hasten the coming of our Lord."

Then shall the minister pray for protection, deliverance from temptation, for an early acceptance of Christ as Saviour and Lord, and a place of service in the will of God.

Benediction. (The usher will escort the parents back to their seat.)

CHURCH MEMBERSHIP

RECEPTION OF MEMBERS

INTRODUCTION

Emphasis upon church membership may be carried to several extremes. Either it may be stressed until quality is sacrificed and quantity becomes the only consideration, or it may be neglected until the united strength of the church is lost in the informal relationship. However, where spiritual standards of eligibility are maintained, a basic procedure is necessary. The following fundamentals can be observed generally, even where there is a denominational procedure to be followed. First, have an established standard of eligibility. The irreducible minimum standard will require satisfactory evidence of regeneration, conformity to the church's beliefs, and acceptance of its constitution and by-laws. Second, have a properly authorized body whose responsibility it is to ascertain eligibility of applicants. The Christian and Missionary Alliance "Suggested Constitution for Churches" provides that "The elders with the Pastor shall constitute the committee on membership." Third, have it required of all applicants that they must be interviewed by this membership committee to determine their eligibility for membership. Such an interview should be pleasant and informal, without sacrificing its purpose. It is a wise policy to use the interview procedure with every applicant. Should denominational practice conflict with the above provisions, the wise pastor can and will fulfill their fundamental aim in a personal visit to each applicant.

THE RECEPTION SERVICE

Members may be received during either a regular worship service or a communion service. The pastor will choose the proper place to include it in the order.

The pastor, announcing the reception of members, will read the names of those being received and the manner of their reception (letter, confession of faith, restatement of faith).

The elders or the properly designated church officials, will come forward and take their place with the pastor in front of the altar.

Ushers previously appointed to the task may escort those being received to a position in front of and facing the pastor and elders, and then be seated.

Portions of the following or other Scripture may be read:

"What shall I render unto the Lord for all his benefits toward me? I will take the cup of salvation, and call upon the name of the Lord. I will pay my vows unto the Lord now in the presence of all his people." Psalm 116:12-14

"For with the heart man believeth unto righteousness; and with the mouth confession is made unto salvation." Romans 10:10

"Whosoever therefore shall confess me before men, him will I confess also before my Father which is in heaven." Matthew 10:32

Or, Acts 19:1-6; 1 Timothy 4:14-16; Hebrews 6:1-2; 1 Peter 1:1-12

Then shall the minister read the following covenant:

"We, the members of this church, do solemnly covenant together with God, and with one another that we will abstain from fleshly lusts which war against the soul; we will be kind to one another, putting away from us all bitterness, anger, wrath, clamor, and evil speaking; and we will be tender-hearted, forgiving one another even as God for Christ's sake hath forgiven us.

"We who are heads of families will observe the worship of God in our homes and will endeavor to lead our children or others committed to our care to a saving knowledge and personal faith in the Lord Jesus Christ. We will attend regularly, so far as Providence permits, the services of worship on the Lord's Day and such other services as the church may appoint. We will observe together the Lord's Supper. We will aid, as the Lord prospers us, in the support of a faithful Christian ministry among us, and in sending the saving Gospel of Christ to the whole human family.

"We will remember those who have the rule over us, esteeming them very highly for their work's sake. For them we will faithfully pray, and with them we will faithfully labor as it may be our privilege.

"God being our helper, this do we covenant to do."

Or, if desired, the following may be used:

"Christian friends, we rejoice in this expression of your desire to unite yourselves with us in this relationship. Because you have witnessed a good confession of faith you are already one with the redeemed people of God of all generations. By uniting with this church you enjoy all its sacred privileges and bear its responsibilities. It is your sacred obligation to uphold its testimony before everyone needing its message; to pray for its success; to give for its support; to attend its services and thus strengthen its ministry. In love, labor, and sacrifice prosper its work, encourage its leaders, and bring daily growth and enrichment to your own soul. Always walk worthy of the name of Christ and His Church, avoiding the very appearance of evil. Love the brethren, and esteem them which be over you in the Lord very highly for their work's sake."

And to the congregation: (Have them stand if desired, or have them stand during the whole reception if desired.)

"Beloved, in receiving these Christian brethren into our fellowship we do enter into solemn covenant and obligation. Let them never find occasion to be ashamed of any of us, nor disappointed by our life or testimony.

May they ever find this House of God a place of spiritual enrichment, encouragement, and refuge. We should always be ready to receive them as brethren, bear their burdens in the love of Christ, and share with them the deepest needs of life. All that the Word of God has led them to expect to find among the redeemed should be found here. We shall, by the grace of God, in receiving them into our fellowship, pledge to them in like manner as we have required them to pledge all that is consistent to a godly life. May our communion be sweet and our joy full."

Brief prayer of dedication.

The right hand of fellowship shall be extended by the minister, or the minister and elders.

Presentation of membership certificate, or Bible, or some suitable token of commemoration.

"Blest Be the Tie That Binds" may be sung at the conclusion if desired. (If ushers have been used, they may now escort the new members to their seats.)

NOTE: The minister will see that the official membership records of the church are properly inscribed with the members' names, correctly spelled, and the date of the occasion.

MEMBERSHIP LETTERS

REQUEST FOR TRANSFER

If the applicant for membership is known to have membership in another church, the courteous thing to do is to suggest that it be transferred. Since most members profess ignorance as to how to go about it, the minister will suggest that he be permitted to write for the letter of transfer. If the applicant himself wishes, possibly for personal reasons, to write for the letter, this is acceptable.

The request for the transfer of membership is available in books of printed forms. However, the minister can accomplish the same thing with a simple letter on the church stationery. It will contain the following elements:

Dear Christian friends:

At the request of *(Mr. John Doe)* I am writing to ask for the transfer of his letter of membership to this church. He (she) has signified his (her) desire to be received into our fellowship at the next reception of members, which is to be soon.

The courtesy of your early reply will be very greatly appreciated.

Cordially yours,

NOTE: Some denominations require that letters requesting or issuing transfer of membership shall be signed by the clerk, or some similar official. The minister may still use his good office to expedite such matters.

ISSUANCE OF TRANSFER

Again, printed forms for this are available, though the following simple form will suffice:

Dear Christian friends:

This is to certify that *(Mr. John Doe)* is a member in good and regular standing, and in full fellowship with this church. As such we commend him (her) to your Christian love and oversight. Membership in this church ceases with the issuance of this letter. (Or, Membership in this church is continued until notified of his reception elsewhere.) (Or, When he (she) shall have so united his (her) connection with us will cease.)

Cordially yours,

INSTALLATION OF OFFICERS

INTRODUCTION

No task rendered in the name and for the glory of the Lord Jesus Christ is small or unimportant. Officials frequently view their place in the church with the attitude, "Somebody has to do it." The essential dignity of being "laborers together with God" must be impressed upon them. A service of installation, if given proper planning and dignity, will make the church's leaders and people alike feel the honor and privilege of working with and for the Lord Jesus Christ. If the minister chooses to preach a sermon on some theme related to office-holding and service, the installation might well follow the message. It may be conducted prior to the serving of Communion, or another place in the worship order may be chosen. He will explain the order of the installation to those involved so they can fulfill his directions without making mistakes. Effort should be made to have the entire staff of newly elected officers present for this occasion. A place is generally reserved for them to sit together near the front of the auditorium.

THE INSTALLATION FOR CHURCH OFFICERS

Hymn: One of the following might be used: "Work for the Night is Coming"; "Jesus Calls

Us"; "In the Service of the King"; "Take My Life and Let It Be."

Scripture: Acts 6: 1-6, or 1 Timothy 3: 1-7, or 1 Timothy 3: 8-17, or 1 Timothy 5: 1, 2, 17-22, or Titus 1: 5-9, or 1 Peter 5: 2-4.

Minister: Ask the officers to stand, either where they are, or if they are few enough in number, they may come forward and take a place in front facing the minister.

"Dearly beloved brethren: You have been chosen to office by the vote of this church. It is my duty to impress upon you the greatness, solemnity, and importance of the work unto which you are chosen. You will take heed unto yourselves, to be examples to the church in your daily living. Take heed also to the flock of God over whom the Holy Spirit has placed you in your office. Give prayerful attention unto the office which is entrusted to you, to fulfill, as unto the Lord Jesus Christ, all its functions. By accepting this trust, you indicate, without reservation, your commitment and loyalty to the message, program, constitution, doctrine, procedures, and world-wide program of The Christian and Missionary Alliance. Be found faithful that you might enter into the joy of the Lord, to whom you shall render an account.

"Do you now accept your office as a sacred and solemn trust from the Lord Jesus Christ, promising Him and this church to fulfill its responsibilities and ministries as indicated above to the best of your ability?"

Officers: Each responding for himself, shall say: "I do."

Minister: "Will you strive with God's help to be examples to the flock in the midst of whom He hast set you as leaders, holding the mystery of the faith in a pure conscience?"

Officers: Each responding for himself, shall say: "I will."

Minister: "Do you, the members of this church, acknowledge and receive these officers, entering with them into the spirit of the vow they have just made to God and this church? Do you promise to honor them, encourage them, co-operate with them, and pray for them, according as the Word of God and the constitution of this church admonishes?

"You will rise to your feet, to signify that you will stand with them in all their labor of love and spiritual oversight."

The congregation will stand.

Minister: "Let us now pray a prayer of dedication, each of you dedicating these leaders to God and to their tasks, and dedicating yourselves afresh to the spiritual unity and progress of this church, under the blessing of Christ the Head of the Church."

Then follows the prayer of dedication by the minister. The regular order of worship will resume at this point, possibly with another hymn.

INSTALLATION FOR SUNDAY-SCHOOL STAFF

It is preferable to use this service during the morning worship, the first Sunday of the Sunday-school year.

Hymn: One of the following might be used: "Jesus Calls Us"; "Take My Life and Let It Be"; "The Call for Reapers"; "My Trust."

Minister: " 'But when he saw the multitudes, he was moved with compassion on them, because they fainted, and were scattered abroad, as sheep having no shepherd. Then saith he unto his disciples, The harvest truly is plenteous, but the laborers are few.' You who have been chosen to labor with the Lord this year in our Sunday school, and who are willing to consecrate your service this day unto Him, will you please stand?"

Sunday-school workers stand and take their place in the front of the auditorium. This is arranged ahead of time.

Minister: "To you as leaders in the Sunday school has been given a task as great as any the church can offer. It is the call of the Great Teacher, who said: 'Ye have not chosen me, but I have chosen you, and ordained you, that ye should go and bring

forth fruit, and that your fruit should remain.' It is the charge of the Word of God
which says, 'Study to shew thyself approved
unto God, a workman that needeth not to be
ashamed.' It is the high privilege of being
'labourers together with God.'

"Will you accept this call to service in our
church as the call of God, indicating without
reservation your commitment and loyalty to
the message, doctrine, constitution, program
and world-wide ministry of The Christian
and Missionary Alliance?"

Teachers and Officers in Unison: "Being
confident of my calling from God, and realizing that I am dealing with eternal souls, I
hereby, covenant before God to dedicate my
life to His service. In humble dependence
upon God I pledge myself to the faithful fulfillment of all my duties, to live a consistent
Christian life and earnestly to endeavor to
be a soul winner, especially among those who
are in my care. I also pledge without reservation my commitment and loyalty to the
message, doctrine, constitution, program, and
world-wide ministry of The Christian and
Missionary Alliance." *(Written copies of the
above will be given the staff ahead of time.)*

Minister: " 'Therefore, my beloved brethren,
be ye stedfast, unmoveable, always abounding in the work of the Lord, forasmuch as ye
know that your labour is not in vain in the

Lord.' 'And he gave some, apostles; and
some, prophets; and some evangelists; and
some, pastors and teachers; For the perfect-
ing of the saints, for the work of the ministry,
for the edifying of the body of Christ.'"
1 Corinthians 15: 58; Ephesians 4: 11, 12.

*Hymn: "Have Thy Way Lord, Have Thy
Way" (one stanza).*

Minister: (To the congregation) "To every
member of the church family may it in very
truth be said of us as we study together in
the Sunday school this coming year, 'Thy
words were found and I did eat them; and
thy word was unto me the joy and rejoicing
of mine heart.' Realizing the nearness of our
Lord's return, and the fields already white
unto harvest, will you join them with your
consecration. 'I beseech you therefore,
brethren, by the mercies of God, that ye present your bodies a living sacrifice, holy, acceptable unto God, which is your reasonable
service.' 'Neither will I offer . . . unto the
Lord my God of that which doth cost me
nothing.'"

Minister: "Let us pray." *Invite congregation to stand. Then follows the prayer of
consecration of the Sunday-school staff and
of the people.*

Hymn: "Fill Me Now."

Benediction: "Now unto him that is able
to do exceeding abundantly above all that

we ask or think, according to the power that
worketh in us, unto him be glory in the
church by Christ Jesus throughout all ages,
world without end.   Amen." Ephesians 3:
20, 21.

INSTALLATION OF A PASTOR

INTRODUCTION

In the light of the holy solemnity and sacred
dignity with which men are set apart to the gospel ministry, it is altogether fitting that a pastor's ministry in a given church be begun in a
similar atmosphere.   The responsibility for his
installation usually rests with a district or sec-
tional official or moderator.   He, together with
the officials of the church, initiates arrangements.
If neighboring pastors are to be invited to participate, he will see that they are contacted, and
specific parts of the service assigned to them.

In cases where the denominational procedure
does not provide for the installation of its pastors, and where it is not the custom of some district official to initiate such a service for the men
under his supervision, the local church itself may
initiate plans for such a service.

The service should be arranged and conducted
within a very short time following the arrival
of the new pastor, preferably on the first Sunday
in his new pulpit.   Where arrangements are being
initiated by the local church, it will determine
whether neighboring pastors are to be invited
and what shall be expected of them, and whether
some representative of the pastors and churches
of the city is to be included in the program.   The
chairman of the church board, or some similar
church official, is generally designated to speak

for the church. More than one spokesman for the church may be chosen if desired, although all departments can be adequately represented by a single speaker. The time for conducting the service will be largely dictated by the custom of the area, as well as by the convenience of the participants. It is preferable that the installation be held as a part of a regular worship service of the church, if convenient. In such a case the usual order of service will prevail, with adjustments suitable to incorporate the essential elements.

The following suggested outline is for the preparation of a simple service devoted entirely to the installation:

The Installation:

Appropriate Hymn(s).

Invocation and Lord's Prayer.

Scripture Lesson or Responsive Reading.

Special Music.

Greetings from ministerial organization—to extend the welcome of the pastors and churches of the city.

Greetings from the church—by chairman of official board.

He will extend the official welcome for the church, making a plea for a happy and spiritually fruitful relationship, pledging the love, loyalty, prayers, and fullest co-operation of the congregation.

Charge to the pastor—by a denominational representative or a chosen pastor.

Special Music.

Charge to the congregation—by a denominational representative or a chosen pastor.

Installation Prayer—by a denominational representative or a chosen pastor.

Brief response by the pastor.
Closing Hymn.
Benediction—by the pastor.

A CONSECRATION SERVICE

(For one going into Christian service.)

INTRODUCTION

Blessed is the church which has many of its sons and daughters called into active Christian service. Quite apart from the more formal ordination or commissioning service, the local congregation will want not only to recognize, but also to "set apart" those who leave to serve. The ties of purpose and fellowship are the richer and the stronger when this is done. Let it be stressed that the purpose of this type of consecration service is not to duplicate or be a substitute for the more formal procedure of ordination. It is an act of simplicity, performed to attach spiritual recognition to the laborer and his task, and to further the church's interest in his life and service. Such a service should be brief, and should avoid any atmosphere of ostentation. It will be most effective when planned as a brief part of the regular order of worship.

The Consecration Service

At the point chosen in the regular order of the service, the minister will announce the consecration service. The one being set apart will be brought to the front by an usher, or may be seated at the front and ready ahead of time. Officers or representatives of every department of the church should also be near the front.

The minister shall read one or more of the following (or other) portions of Scripture: Exodus 33: 12-18; Nehemiah 8: 1-3, 5-6, 8; Acts 12: 2-3.

Then he shall say: "*(John Doe) or (Jane Doe),* will you now stand before this people and declare unto them the call of God upon your life and the purpose for which you go forth to serve?"

This will afford the Christian worker an opportunity of brief testimony, and an appeal for the interest and prayer support of his home church.

Then shall the minister say: "Who of this congregation is willing to give to *(John Doe) (Jane)* your expression of Christian thankfulness for his (her) call into active service, your vote of encouragement in his (her) undertaking, your promise of loving support and faithful prayer? Let him who is willing stand to his feet." *The congregation will stand.*

Then shall the minister say: "*(John) (Jane)* I now ask you to kneel here, while the officers of this church join me in laying hands upon you and praying the prayer of consecration over you as a servant of the Lord called forth from this congregation."

The prayer of consecration shall follow.
Then the minister may present to the person thus consecrated some token of the church's esteem and continuing interest, if this is desired.
A hymn may be sung in conclusion.

A GROUND BREAKING CEREMONY

INTRODUCTION

Inasmuch as this is an outdoor service it should be accommodated to weather conditions. The time of service must also be adjusted to the convenience of the congregation. If the place where the ceremony is to be held is next door, or near to the house of worship, it is generally best to plan the ground breaking in conjunction with a regular gathering of the people at the church. The order of service should be mimeographed or printed and distributed to all present so they can participate. The people should be urged to move in close together and near the designated spot of the ceremony, as it may be difficult to hear well out of doors.

The Ceremony

> Scripture: One of the following, or other passages might be read: 1 Chronicles 21:22-26, or 1 Chronicles 22:11-16, 19, or 2 Chronicles 2:1-9, or Ezra 7:11-26, or Psalm 24, or Psalm 29, or Psalm 34, or Isaiah 12.
> Invocation and Lord's Prayer.
> Responsive Reading—from printed sheets prepared in advance, or from hymnal.
> Hymn or Special Music—this will be limited to very familiar music if an instrument is not available.
> Brief remarks—by minister or guest speaker, as to the building to be erected and the aim for its use as a House of God, educational unit, parish house, or parsonage.
> Ground Breaking—The minister (or some especially selected or honored person) will take the shovel and remove the first shovelful of

earth. Other officers and leaders of the
church may be designated to follow, each
removing a shovelful of earth.
Prayer—for the furtherance of this undertaking that it might be to the glory of God and
the good of men.
Hymn or Special Music.
Benediction

LAYING A CORNERSTONE

INTRODUCTION

This is an important moment in the experience
of a congregation, and by proper care and dignity in planning there will be attached to it
spiritual significance consistent to the occasion.
Contents of the box in the cornerstone will be
determined and prepared beforehand. All persons taking part in the ceremony will be instructed as to what to do. Preferably, printed
or mimeographed copies of the order of service,
Scriptures, and hymns will be prepared for distribution to all present.

Laying the Cornerstone

Doxology.
Invocation and Lord's Prayer.
Hymn: Such as: "Holy, Holy, Holy"; "How
Firm a Foundation"; "The Church's One
Foundation"; "Rock of Ages."
Scripture: One or more of the following, or
other passages may be selected:

Isaiah 28:16	Ephesians 4:11-16
Psalm 118:22, 23	Matthew 7:24-27
Ezra 3:10-13	1 Corinthians 3:10-17
Ephesians 2:19-22	1 Peter 2:4-8

Prayer: Possibly by a guest minister, chairman of the building committee, a leading elder, or chairman of the trustee board.

Special Music: Bear in mind that it is difficult to hear well out-of-doors. Instrumental music might be best.

Brief Remarks: By the minister or guest chosen for the occasion.

Laying the Cornerstone: By the minister. He will have consulted the building contractor for instructions about putting on the mortar and setting the stone. Contents of the cornerstone will be announced, which generally includes a Bible, history of the church, accurate membership roll, list of officers, trustees, and building committee, and possibly even an honor roll of the contributors who are making the building possible.

Prayer of Thanksgiving: For present and continued progress in building; for the safety of those who labor; for the ultimate fulfillment of the purpose for which the structure is being built.

Hymn.

Benediction.

DEDICATING A BUILDING

THE CHURCH

INTRODUCTION

No other hour in a church's history quite compares with the crowning achievement of dedicating a new building. Nor does any other service find itself provided with such enthusiastic anticipation. Such a service, to be worthy of all the factors that have brought it about, must seek to capture the spirit of exultation which is naturally present, and direct it to the highest spiritual plane. The burning vision, the tireless labors, the spirit of sacrifice, thanksgiving to God, love and loyalty to Christ and His Church are all elements to be considered.

There is no guide as to what limits should govern the planning of a dedicatory service, except that of good taste and sensible length. Some congregations want all their former pastors to be invited to participate. Others want all the Christian organizations of the community to be represented. Still others will think every department of the church should be included. Obviously, the program can thus become quite complicated as well as lengthy. The minister will show consideration for the desires of all concerned, and attempt to arrive at a happy and acceptable solution. Doubtless a representative could be included from all groups indicated as well as official representation from the denomination.

As important as making the choice of who shall be included in the program is the fact that each one be properly instructed as to the part he is to have.

It is highly important to have the entire service printed or mimeographed, being careful to include the responses to be made, the act of dedication, and possibly even the words of the hymns to be sung.

THE DEDICATION SERVICE

The following outline is meant to be a general guide for preparing the order of service, and instructing those having part in it.

Prelude: (Organ, Piano, or Orchestra).

Hymn: "All Hail the Power" (Congregation standing).

The Call to Worship:

Minister—"Who shall ascend into the hill of the Lord?
Or who shall stand in his holy place?"

Congregation—"He that hath clean hands, and a pure heart;
Who hath not lifted up his soul unto vanity,
Nor sworn deceitfully."

Minister—"He shall receive the blessing from the Lord
And righteousness from the God of his salvation.
This is the generation of them that seek him,
That seek thy face, O Jacob."

Congregation—"Lift up your heads, O ye gates;
And be ye lifted up, ye everlasting doors;
And the King of glory shall come in."

Minister—"Who is the King of glory?"

Congregation—"The Lord of Hosts,
He is the King of glory."

Invocation and Lord's Prayer.

Scripture: One or more of the following, or other passages may be selected: 2 Chronicles 6; Psalm 84: 1-4, 10-12; Psalm 24; Ephesians 2: 20-22; 1 Peter 2: 1-10.

Special Music (choir or soloist): "Bless This House"—or a similar number.

Recognitions and Acknowledgments: (One of the following may be chosen, either the "Trustee" part, or the "Presentation of the Keys.")

The minister addresses the trustees:

"You have been selected by the members of this church to fill the responsible positions of trustees of this House of Worship, now being dedicated to the service of Almighty God. You will at all times, when you represent this church, act on its behalf and for its welfare.

"God's holy temple is a sacred place in which He is to be worshiped in the beauty of holiness and love. Nothing should enter this sacred place that would defile it.

"Protect it at all times; preserve it for continual service; improve it as needs and opportunities arise. To you is committed the task of keeping it worthy of its name, the House of God.

"From this time forth, because of your authority, you will hold this property in trust for God and this church. May Christian faith and hope and love dwell in your hearts, and may the Holy Spirit guide and direct you in all the activities that fall within the sphere of your responsibility as the Board of Trustees."

The Trustees' Covenant:

"We, the Board of Trustees of this church, do covenant with God and with one another to discharge our duties faithfully and to hold this House of Worship, and trust that it may, at all times, magnify the preaching of the Word of God and thus fulfill its mission to this community for all the purposes for which it is now being set apart."

Or, Presentation of the Keys.

The chairman of the building committee (or contractor) will make a speech of presentation outlining the financial investment represented by the building and all pertinent facts of its construction, and then present the keys to the minister or chairman of the trustees. The appropriate person will accept the keys with a response.

The Act of Dedication:

Minister—"To the Glory of God the Father, to the honor of the Lord Jesus Christ His only begotten Son our Saviour, and to the praise of the Holy Spirit our Comforter;"

Congregation—"We dedicate this House."

Minister—"For worship in prayer and praise; For the ministry of the Word of God; For the celebration of the Church's ordinances;

6

For the guidance of childhood and the sanctification of the family;"

Congregation—"We dedicate this House."

Minister—"For comfort to those who mourn;
For strength to those who are weak;
For help to those who are tempted;
For instruction in the ways of righteousness;"

Congregation—"We dedicate this House."

Minister—"For the teaching of the doctrines of our church;
For the seeking of the salvation of mankind;
For the witnessing of Christ's saving Gospel to the uttermost parts of the earth;
In the hope of the soon appearing of our glorious Lord and coming King;"

Minister and Congregation together—
"To God the Father, God the Son and God the Holy Ghost, eternal, holy and glorious Trinity, three Persons, one God, to Thee:
We dedicate this church."

Prayer of Dedication.
Hymn: "The Church's One Foundation."
Congratulations of Former Pastors.
Special Music.
Dedicatory Sermon.
Closing Hymn.
Benediction.

The Act of Dedication:

Minister—"Because we have purposed in our hearts to build a sanctuary to the worship of the true and living God, and to the service of Jesus Christ our Lord, I call upon this congregation to stand for the holy act of dedication.

"To the glory of God the Father; to the honor of Jesus Christ the Son; to the praise of the Holy Spirit—"

Congregation—"We dedicate this House."

Minister—"Knowing there is none other name under heaven given among men whereby we must be saved—"

Congregation—"We dedicate this House to the bringing of the saving knowledge of our Lord Jesus Christ to the unconverted."

Minister—"In obedience to the explicit command of Christ to go into all the world and preach the Gospel to every creature—"

Congregation—"We dedicate this House to the world-wide task of the whole Church of Christ, till all the kingdoms of this world become the Kingdom of our Lord and of His Christ."

Minister—"Realizing the obligation to bring up our children in the nurture and admonition of the Lord—"

Congregation—"We dedicate this House to the sanctity of the home and the hallowing of family life; to the religious nurture and education of children, youth, and adults; to the grace of Christian character, and the warmth of Christian fellowship."

Minister—"In obedience to the command of Christ to love our neighbors as ourselves—"

Congregation—"We dedicate this House to the communion of saints, to the refuge of weary restless souls, to the peace and hope of the oppressed, to the comfort of those that mourn, and to the happiness of all those of like precious faith."

Minister and Congregation Together—"We, the members and friends of this church, deeply grateful for the heritage that has been entrusted to us, and keenly conscious of those ties by which we are bound to the Lord of all life, and to each other, do covenant together in this act of dedication, offering ourselves anew to the work and worship of our Heavenly Father, through Jesus Christ our Lord. Amen."

Prayer of Dedication.
Closing Hymn (may be a hymn of dedication).
Benediction.
Postlude.

AN ALTERNATE CEREMONY

Prelude.

Hymn: "God of Our Fathers" (may be used as processional hymn).

Call to Worship:

Minister—Surely the Lord is in this place.

Congregation—This is none other but the house of God.

Minister—I will lift up my voice in the sanctuary.

Congregation—I will praise Him with songs of gladness, who is the rock of my salvation.

Minister—O come, let us worship and bow down; let us kneel before the Lord our maker.

Congregation—For He is our God; and we are people of His pasture, and the sheep of His hand.

Invocation and Lord's Prayer.

Words of Greeting and Announcements.

Scripture Reading.

Special Music.

The Dedication Sermon—(This may be delivered following the act of dedication if preferred.)

Receiving of Offerings and Gifts.

Offertory.

Choir or other special music.

Presentation of the Building:

Statement by the minister.

Presentation of the building by the contractor to the architect.

Presentation of the building by the architect to building committee.

Presentation of the building by the building committee or trustees (or Official Board).

THE PARSONAGE OR A CHRISTIAN HOME

Introduction

The relationship between the Children of Israel and their God in the matter of devoted things is beautiful to contemplate. Opportunity was afforded to set apart their homes, families, fields, flocks, and goods as devoted to God, thus becoming the objects of His care and blessing.

Equal privilege rests upon the child of grace. And the importance of the home in the economy of God makes it altogether fitting that even the dwelling itself shall be peculiarly set apart unto the Lord. Such devotion and dedication to God shall surely have the salutary effect of strengthening and preserving the sanctity of the Christian home. Thus, let the church set the example in dedicating its parsonage when it buys or builds; and thus let the congregation be encouraged, when they buy or build, to set their homes and dwellings apart to God. Such a service can prove to be of untold blessing to all concerned.

The Ceremony

At the time appointed, the persons invited being assembled, the service may be begun with an appropriate hymn sung by selected singers or the entire company.

Brief Invocation.

Special Music—a soloist or group might sing "Bless This House" or some similarly fitting number. In the absence of singers the words might be read by the minister.

Then shall the minister say:

"Dearly beloved members of this household, and guests: We are assembled here to dedicate this dwelling unto God as a Christian home. It is our hope and our faith that it shall be a place of happiness, adding to life's meaning for all who shall call it 'home.'

"Home was the first institution which God our Father established for His children. Before the church and before any form of civil government, the home was a divine institution. Love was the first bond which linked human lives together, and the home was its expression. The home became the nursery of true faith, of education, of civilization, of culture, of beauty; in short, of all progress. In all the advance of life, the home is still the greatest of human institutions and the most vital expression of the presence of God.

"The home is the place where we find protection from the elements; where food is prepared for nourishment and where beds are provided for rest from the wearying tasks of life. Home is likewise a symbol of the heavenly home which our Lord has gone to prepare for all His redeemed ones. We have 'an house not made with hands, eternal in the heavens,' prepared for us. In this service we now dedicate this home to the Christian ideals for which it was intended, to happiness and peace, and to faith in God through our Lord Jesus Christ. 'Except the Lord build the house, they labor in vain that build it.' "

The minister shall take bread from the table, and breaking it, he shall give a piece to the head of the home, and either give another piece to an invited guest or retain it himself, saying:

"One of the most primitive acts of hospitality is the sharing of bread. To break bread together so that two or more persons partake of the same loaf, thus being nourished by the same food, was a symbol of the common life which they shared. The most familiar prayer among Christian people is found in the petition: 'Give us this day our daily bread.' "

The following sentences and responses (copies prepared for all present) shall be used by the minister, the household and assembled guests:

Minister—"In the love of strength and beauty, in confidence in its good foundations, and the strength of its timbers,"

Response—"We dedicate this house."

Minister—"With a prayer that it be protected from fire, and storm, and all manner of calamity,"

Response—"We dedicate this house."

Minister—"With thanks to God for the beauty of light to shine through its windows, and the beauty of trees and flowers, seas and mountains to surround it,"

Response—"We dedicate this house."

Minister—"With joy in our door which opens to those who knock, with joy in friends who share our provisions,"

Response—"We dedicate this house."

Minister—"To all the sweetness and hallowed joys of home life, to all the hopes of future happiness through God's unmeasured gift of the years,"

Response—"We dedicate this house."

Minister—"To the glory of Jesus Christ as Saviour, and to His honor as Head of this home,"

Response—"We dedicate this house."

Benediction—"The Lord bless us and keep us, the Lord cause His face to shine upon us and be gracious unto us; the Lord lift up the light of His countenance upon us, and give us His peace, this day and evermore. Amen."

LIFTING A DEDICATION

INTRODUCTION

There comes the happy moment in the growth and development of many congregations when new and larger quarters must be built. In most cases this involves a move to a new location. The old property which must be disposed of sometimes is acquired by another religious body, a lodge, or some commercial interest. Since the premises are to be no longer occupied by their former owners, nor used for their specific purposes, it is fitting that their act of dedication be revoked.

The lifting of the dedication will, therefore, include the removal of the cornerstone and its contents, the removal of the church's name and identifying insignia, and everything sacred to its usage. Thus, in a spiritual sense at least, will be lifted and moved to the new place of abode, the memories and attachments of the old.

The ceremony for the lifting of the dedication should follow the last service in the building, if possible. The cornerstone will have been loosened from its mortar so it can be easily and quickly removed during the ceremony. All participants in the service will have been carefully instructed by the minister as to what they are to do and when they are to do it. Though the service is quite brief, the entire order should be printed and distributed to all present so they can take part.

The Ceremony.

Remarks—(by the pastor).

Pastor—" 'And, thou, Lord, in the beginning hast laid the foundation of the earth; and the heavens are the works of thine hands. They shall perish; but thou remainest; and they all shall wax old as doth a garment; And as a vesture shalt thou fold them up, and they shall be changed: but thou art the same, and thy years shall not fail.'" Heb. 1: 10-12.

Congregation—"As the earth and the heavens shall be set aside when they in God's wisdom have served their purposes, so we would set aside this house as having served its useful purpose as our place of worship."

Pastor—"Concerning the law of devoted things we read in Lev. 27: 14, 15, 'And when a man shall sanctify his house to be holy unto the Lord, then the priest shall estimate it, . . . And if he that sanctified it will redeem his house, then he shall add the fifth part of the money of thy estimation unto it and it shall be his.'"

Congregation—"As Israel was allowed to redeem devoted things and the proceeds of the redemption price used to the good of the sanctuary, so the money realized in the sale of this building shall go toward the building of a more appropriate place of worship."

Pastor—"Because that Thou, O Lord, hast enabled this people in faith to move forward toward acquiring a more appropriate place of worship, we therefore lift the dedication of this building in the name of the Father, and of the Son, and of the Holy Ghost."

Trustees—"We, the Board of Trustees of this church, will no longer hold this property in trust for God and this congregation."

(Here the trustees remove the cornerstone)

"This cornerstone, symbol of Christ, the true foundation and cornerstone of His Church, we have removed that it may serve as a token to all that this building will no longer be recognized as our house of prayer and worship."

Congregation—"We thank Thee, O Lord, for the ...... years of blessing in this place; for the pastors, evangelists and missionaries who here have ministered Thy Word; for all the sacred memories attached to this place; for the salvation of souls and the sanctification of believers; for the fellowship of the saints; and for Thy Holy Presence which has attended us in this place of worship. For all these and Thy many blessings we do truly give Thee thanks."

Pastor—"Having been challenged by the opportunities and the great responsibilities that our city presents, and recognizing the need of widening our horizon in effective service for Christ and the salvation of men, we dedicate ourselves and our possessions to the cause of Christ in this community. We shall go forward in the name of Christ, and in faith, asking and expecting great things from God."

Closing Prayer.

Hymn—"Blest Be the Tie That Binds."

BURNING A MORTGAGE

INTRODUCTION

Involvement in debt is a common and sometimes unavoidable experience in the progress of a congregation. Under the best of circumstances, it is a burden from which they are happy to be released. Therefore, the day the mortgage is burned will rank among the outstanding events of their history. It is a matter of local preference whether this event shall be observed at a special service, or incorporated in the order of a regular service. A wide variety of persons may be included in the participation. One, or all, of the original note-signers may be included if available; one representative or officer from each department of the church may be chosen; or former pastors might be invited; or it may be desired that officials of the denomination be invited.

One thing is important to remember: the burning of the mortgage entails what is considered a fire hazard. Safety instructions may be obtained from the local fire marshal's office. Metal vessels should be provided in which to burn the document. The document may be divided into several strips, each being held and ignited by

those participating. Or they may each hold a
lighted taper, applying the flame to the document
at the same time. It may be simplest to have one
individual do the burning. (IMPORTANT NOTE:
Never burn the original mortgage document. It
should be carefully preserved among the church's
valuable papers for legal security. A copy should
be used for the burning ceremony.)

The Ceremony

Participants may assemble on the platform
during the singing of a hymn, if not there before the appointed time in the service.

Scripture or Responsive Reading.

Prayer.

Remarks—usually reminiscent of the events of
   the church's history leading up to the present moment. The number of persons who
   speak and the time allotted will necessarily
   be brief if this ceremony is part of a regular
   service. The minister will usually summar-
   ize the event in his remarks.

Mortgage burning—either as a whole or in
   parts by those designated.

Doxology—Congregation standing.

Closing Prayer.

(The above order may be expanded by additional music and extended remarks if the ceremony is to be celebrated as a special service.)

For more copies of
The Pastor's Handbook
or information on other titles
contact your local Christian
bookstore or call
Christian Publications, toll-free,
1-800-233-4443.